Biggest, Baddest Books

BIGGEST, BADDEST BOOK OF

SEA CREATURES

JEN SCHOELLER

Consulting Editor, Liz Salzmann, M.A./Reading Specialist

Super Sandcastle

An Imprint of Abdo Publishing
www.abdopublishing.com

www.abdopublishing.com

Published by Abdo Publishing, a division of ABDO, PO Box 398166, Minneapolis, Minnesota 55439. Copyright © 2015 by Abdo Consulting Group, Inc. International copyrights reserved in all countries. No part of this book may be reproduced in any form without written permission from the publisher. Super SandCastle™ is a trademark and logo of Abdo Publishing.

Printed in the United States of America, North Mankato, Minnesota
102014
012015

Editor: Alex Kuskowski
Content Developer: Nancy Tuminelly
Interior Design and Production: Jen Schoeller, Mighty Media, Inc.
Photo Credits: Shutterstock, Wikipedia Commons

Library of Congress Cataloging-in-Publication Data

Schoeller, Jen, author.
 Biggest, baddest book of sea creatures / Jen Schoeller.
   pages cm. -- (Biggest, baddest books)
 ISBN 978-1-62403-517-3
1. Marine animals--Juvenile literature. I. Title.
 QL122.2.S355 2015
 591.77--dc23
                2014024010

Super SandCastle™ books are created by a team of professional educators, reading specialists, and content developers around five essential components—phonemic awareness, phonics, vocabulary, text comprehension, and fluency—to assist young readers as they develop reading skills and strategies and increase their general knowledge. All books are written, reviewed, and leveled for guided reading, early reading intervention, and Accelerated Reader® programs for use in shared, guided, and independent reading and writing activities to support a balanced approach to literacy instruction.

CONTENTS

UNDER THE SEA

The ocean covers most of the Earth. In some places the ocean is 33,000 feet (10,058 m) deep! There is a lot of room for sea creatures.

ANIMALS
IN THE OCEAN

There are millions of animals in the ocean.

There are very tiny sea creatures. Some can only be seen under a microscope. There are also huge sea creatures.

MOLLUSKS

Most mollusks have hard shells. Snails and clams are mollusks.

FISH

Fish breathe through gills. Sharks and eels are fish.

CRUSTACEANS

Crustaceans have skeletons on the outside of their bodies. Shrimps and crabs are crustaceans.

PROTOZOANS

Protozoans are very tiny. They only have one cell. Amoebas and ciliates are protozoans.

ECHINODERMS

Echinoderms have five sections. Starfish and sand dollars are echinoderms.

SPONGES

Water flows through sponges. It brings food and oxygen. Sponges can change their shape.

SUPERSIZED
sea creatures

BLUE WHALE
The blue whale is the largest animal that ever existed. It is bigger than the biggest dinosaur! Blue whales can be 98 feet (30 m) long.

Humphead Wrasse

Wrasses are a family of fish. The biggest is the humphead wrasse. It can grow longer than 7.5 feet (2.2 m). The hump on its head never stops growing.

Manta Ray

Manta rays are also called devil rays. They are the largest kind of ray. They can be 23 feet (7 m) wide.

Japanese Spider Crab

The Japanese spider crab is the largest **arthropod**. Its claws can reach 12 feet (3.7 m) apart.

TOXIC KILLERS

STONEFISH

LOCATION: *coasts of the Indian Ocean, Indonesia, northern Australia, Florida, and the Caribbean*

The stonefish is the most **venomous** fish. The **venom** is in its top fin. It looks like a rock. It hides in plain sight on the sea floor.

PUFFER FISH

LOCATION: *oceans near the equator*

Puffer fish are the most **poisonous** fish. They have poison in their organs. They can fill their stomachs with water. This makes them puff up. They look bigger.

8

BLUE-RINGED OCTOPUS

LOCATION: *Indian Ocean and the Pacific Ocean from Japan to Australia*

Blue-ringed octopuses are very **venomous.** They bite their prey. That's how they **inject** the venom. They have 50 to 60 rings. When they are upset, their rings turn bright blue.

BEARDED FIREWORM

LOCATION: *Mediterranean Sea, Atlantic Ocean, and Caribbean Sea.*

The bearded fireworm has **bristles.** The bristles have venom. The worm stings anything that attacks it. The bristles break off and grow back.

SHARK ATTACK!

SHARKS HAVE BEEN AROUND LONGER THAN 400 MILLION YEARS.

Sharks have many rows of teeth. Their teeth are always falling out. Then they grow new teeth.

GREAT WHITE SHARK

Great white sharks live in every ocean. They stay near the coasts. They have bitten more people than any other shark.

TIGER SHARK

Tiger sharks live near the equator. Young tiger sharks have stripes. Their stripes fade as they get older.

HAMMERHEAD SHARK

Hammerhead sharks have heads shaped like hammers. That's how they got their name. They swim in schools during the day. They hunt alone at night.

THE INVISIBLE SQUID

BOBTAIL SQUID

LOCATION: *Pacific Ocean, Indian Ocean, and the coast of South Africa*

The Bobtail squid has a special light organ. Bacteria grow in the light organ. The bacteria produce light. The light matches the light above the squid. This makes the squid hard to see. The squid can also use the light to hunt at night.

GIANT CLAM

The giant clam is a large mollusk. It can be more than 50 inches (127 cm) long.

Its shell has a **hinge**. There are large folds on each side. Adult giant clams cannot close their shells all the way. Giant clams stay on the sea floor. They don't move around.

A GIANT CLAM HAS A HOLE CALLED A SIPHON. IT LETS WATER FLOW IN AND OUT.

LIVING OOZE

SEA CUCUMBERS

LOCATION: *Indian Ocean, Atlantic Ocean, Pacific Ocean, Mediterranean Sea*

Sea cucumbers can make their bodies soft. This lets them fit into very small spaces. Then they harden their bodies. This holds them in place.

Sea cucumbers throw sticky threads at predators. They can also turn some of their organs to liquid. They shoot them out when they are scared. Then the organs grow back.

Colorful CAMOUFLAGE

CAMOUFLAGE IS WHEN AN ANIMAL MATCHES ITS SURROUNDINGS. THIS MAKES IT HARD FOR PREDATORS TO SEE IT.

MIMIC OCTOPUS

The mimic octopus can change shape. It can look like other sea animals.

COLEMAN SHRIMP

Coleman shrimp live on fire urchins. The urchins protect the shrimp.

SOFT CORAL CRAB

Soft coral crabs live on coral **reefs.** They change color to match the reef.

15

STARGAZERS

Stargazers are fish. Their eyes are on top of their heads. Their mouths also face up. They bury themselves in the sea floor. Only their eyes show. They wait for prey to swim above them. Then they leap up to grab the prey.

SPOTTED STARGAZER

FRECKLED STARGAZER

NORTHERN STARGAZER

SMALL BUT SIGNIFICANT

COPEPODS

Copepods are tiny crustaceans. Millions of copepods live all over the world. They are very important. Many sea creatures need them for food.

Sea Slugs

N udibranchs are mollusks. But they don't have shells. They are very colorful.

SEA SLUG EGGS

Nudibranchs lay eggs in ribbons. Some ribbons only have a few eggs. Some have thousands of eggs.

FLABELLINA
AEOLID

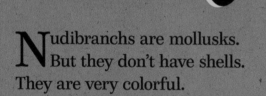

NEMBROTHA
DORID

There are two main types of nudibranchs. They are dorids and aeolids. A dorid breathes through a gill on its back. It looks like a flower. An aeolid has many hair-like parts. They help it breathe.

SANGUINEUS
DORID

HYPSELODORIS
DORID

GLAUCUS
AEOLID

ARCHIDORIS
DORID

CRATENA
AEOLID

19

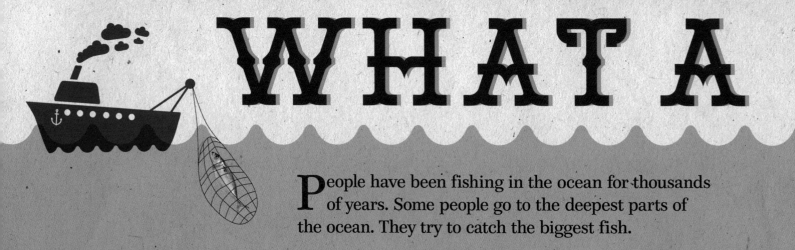

WHAT A

P eople have been fishing in the ocean for thousands of years. Some people go to the deepest parts of the ocean. They try to catch the biggest fish.

OARFISH

The giant oarfish is the largest bony fish. One washed onto the beach near San Diego, California. It was 23 feet (7 m) long.

DEEPEST CATCH

A type of cusk eel lives in deeper water than any other fish. One was caught in the Puerto Rico Trench. It was 27,460 feet (8,370 m) deep.

CATCH!

GOLIATH GROUPER

Goliath groupers live near coral **reefs**. They can reach very large sizes, growing up to 9.84 feet (3 m) and can weigh as much as 790 pounds (360 kg).

OCEAN SUNFISH

The ocean sunfish is the heaviest bony fish. A really huge one was caught in 1910. It was about 3,500 pounds (1,588 kg).

CREATURES FROM THE DEEP

BLACK SWALLOWER

The black swallower lives up to 9,000 feet (2,743 m) deep. A black swallower's stomach can stretch. It can eat fish that are bigger than it is.

ATLANTIC WOLFFISH

The Atlantic wolffish lives near the sea floor. It likes rocky areas. It is found more than 1,000 feet (305 m) deep.

FANGTOOTH

The fangtooth is found up to 16,500 feet (5,029 m) deep. It has very big teeth.

WHAT DO YOU KNOW ABOUT SEA CREATURES?

1. A BLUE-RINGED OCTOPUS HAS 50 TO 60 RINGS. **TRUE OR FALSE?**

2. GIANT CLAMS MOVE AROUND A LOT. **TRUE OR FALSE?**

3. SOFT CORAL CRABS NEVER CHANGE COLOR. **TRUE OR FALSE?**

4. THERE ARE TWO MAIN TYPES OF NUDIBRANCHS. **TRUE OR FALSE?**

ANSWERS: 1) TRUE 2) FALSE 3) FALSE 4) TRUE

23

ARTHROPOD – an animal that has a shell instead of a backbone and at least six legs. Insects, spiders, and crabs are arthropods.

BRISTLE – a short, stiff hair or something similar to a hair.

HINGED – having a joint that allows two attached parts to swing back and forth.

INJECT – to use something sharp, such as a tooth or a stinger, to force a liquid into something.

POISONOUS – containing something that can injure or kill when touched or eaten.

REEF – a strip of coral, rock, or sand that is near the surface of the ocean.

SPECIES – a group of related living beings.

VENOM – a poison produced by some animals that is injected into prey by biting or stinging. If something has venom, it is *venomous*